Empirical Evidence

EMPIRICAL EVIDENCE

POEMS BY
STEVE KRONEN

THE UNIVERSITY OF GEORGIA PRESS

ATHENS AND LONDON

© 1992 by Steve Kronen

All rights reserved

Published by the University of Georgia Press

Athens, Georgia 30602

Designed by Betty P. McDaniel

Set in 10½ on 13½ Berkeley Old Style Medium

by G&S Typesetters, Inc.

Printed and bound by Thomson-Shore, Inc.

The paper in this book meets the guidelines for
permanence and durability of the Committee on
Production Guidelines for Book Longevity of the
Council on Library Resources.

Printed in the United States of America

96 95 94 93 92   C   5 4 3 2 1

96 95 94 93 92   P   5 4 3 2 1

Library of Congress Cataloging in Publication Data

Kronen, Steve.

Empirical evidence : poems / by Steve Kronen.

p.   cm.

ISBN 0-8203-1476-5 (alk. paper).

—ISBN 0-8203-1477-3 (pbk. : alk. paper)

I. Title.

PS3561.R585E46   1992

811'.54—dc20   92-8236

CIP

British Library Cataloging in Publication Data available

For my wife, Ivonne,
my parents, Phil and Jan, and my brother Lar

Acknowledgments

Grateful acknowledgment is made to the following publications in whose pages these poems—many of which have since been revised—first appeared.

American Poetry Review: "Aleister Crowley Meets with the American Theosophists, Philadelphia, 1908," "The Island of Glassblowers"
American Scholar: "A Scientist Aboard the Titanic Says Good-Bye to His Wife in His Head"
Boulevard: "Mayflies"
Georgia Review: "Owl and Mouse in a Cage"
Massachusetts Review: "Tolstoy on the Train to Astapovo"
Missouri Review: "The Road-Gang Is Served Supper at a Country Inn"
Palmetto Review: "Passenger Pigeons," "Moving Away"
Ploughshares: "The Reverend Falwell Describes the Bakkers' Swimming Pool," "Think of the Blackouts"
Prairie Schooner: "Natural History," "This Afternoon"
River Styx: "An Incident at Andersonville—from the Recollections of Private Charles Hopkins," "Your Voice"
Shenandoah: "The Lepers Who Tend the Hothouse Flowers"
Southern Review: "Married Woman," "Near and Far," "A Short History of Christianity"
Threepenny Review: "After Viewing Twelve Versions of Madonna and Child," "For L, Born August 6, 1945"
Yellow Silk: "The Fishermen Pull Their Boats In," "Lament," "Asleep Together"

I would very much like to thank Ron DeMaris, Jeffrey Harrison, Larry Apple, and Paul Sanz for their support and encouragement, and deepest thanks to Peter Schmitt for his necessary, unstinting help and friendship. Much appreciation to Frank Rakoncay for his talent and generosity. Also, a heartfelt thanks to Heather McHugh. And much thanks to the Florida Arts Council for its very generous support.

Contents

I

After Viewing Twelve Versions
of Madonna and Child

So often they look not like infants
But little men, heads disproportionate
And nothing yielding in the eyes
Which are possessed of a slight

Exasperation or boredom.
If they were born several centuries later,
You could see them placing phone calls
To their brokers or wearing black homburgs

In a smoky room. It must be faith then
That propels us to worship, as if
Adoration could absolve our
So often coming up short: of kindness,

Of compassion, of whatever it takes
To fill in the blank spaces of our hearts.
Such faith helped fill the backgrounds of the portraits:
Fat-cheeked cherubs no older than their charge,

Or winged teenagers whose luminous
Complexions attest to the virtues
Of a permanently deferred puberty.
Occasionally a farmer can be seen

Plowing a rocky pasture, gray boulders
Rising behind him. His hands are calloused
From his hard work and were he to rub
The baby's cheek, the infant would have to cry.

*

3

And the mother, not much older
Than a cheerleader, would try to shush him,
Try to distract him with the beads that hang
Between her small breasts grown so tender

With the sudden milk. *There now,* she says,
There now, shifting his small miraculous bulk
From shoulder to shoulder. But for now
The baby's fine, stands in her lap,

Sure-footed and undaunted, his spine
Able to bear his precocious antics
As he stares directly at us, out toward
The centuries gathered before him like a crowd

At a county fair, who, thick-lidded and happy,
Nod their amazed admiration
For the man who guesses weights and who
Hasn't been wrong all morning.

Natural History

for El in her pregnancy

This is how the birds make fossils:
They lie down carefully into the waiting plane of rock
Leaving themselves.
All memory, gene, and sorrow
Register into the gray hillside
The way an echo remains in the cave of the ear
After the thunder has gone.
It is how we etch our histories
Beneath each other's tongues
And are able to recognize one another in the dark
Marvelling at the blossoms of our hands
And how they turn always toward
A source of warmth.

The brain is incapable of such calculations.
When any two bodies are pressed this closely,
Some transformation must occur—
Wine, or water, or the soul's unrelenting intaglio
Into flesh, marrow

Pushing outward to its own white outline.
Think of the fever of birth
Surrounding you like a halo
And how it burns into the air around you
Changing the pressure in the room
As if a storm were ascending,
Like Elijah, full-bodied,
Leaving this Earth for the last time

More easily than he entered.
When you stretch in your sleep
And something in you aches

Like a phantom limb,
Palpable, charged, wholly awake;
It is me, somewhere in this city
Stretching too behind my scrim
Of sleep. I dream of you and the baby in you
And how, yes, nature abhors a vacuum,
For look how we manage to fill whatever void presents itself,
Learning bone by bone
Each earthly act of love.

Press softly upon the baby's crown
Where the sutures meet like Samaritan roads
And the thumb will fill this delicate depression
Where dreams form
Before they become dreams.
There is no well deeper than this, no wish
More indelible.

The Lepers Who Tend
the Hothouse Flowers

They come to their work the way a girl
approaches a horse she loves, and peel
from the healthy stalks the dead
and dying leaves. Their eyes turn away
from the new arrival who, still dazed
with the diagnosis, somnambulates
inland away from the disappearing
ship. Others retrieve his luggage
before the tide engulfs it whole.

Yet in a year, he also begins
the process of forgetting.
His surroundings evoke his admiration.
The places on earth are few, he learns,
where temperatures are moderate enough
and rainy days so fairly meted
that so many flowers grow with such
luxury and little effort. When still
a boy he pictured adult life like this:
not the situation, but
the tone behind the situation;
acres of every thinkable color
growing toward the serene sky
that passed beyond the glass roofs.

At night the waters charge the bluffs
and he can gauge the passing hours
by their cadence. This lulls him to a sleep
in which he is always immaculate,

and this body, the one he wears daily,
is seamless and full of light. In time
his former life refuses to adhere,
is left behind like gossip and seems
no more than the lattice of a dried leaf,
a lace shawl thrown around
a pair of bony shoulders.

Beneath his bed is a chest of scarves,
as sheer and various as the flowers,
the silk soothing to the suppurated
skin. Each Friday night these men
and women clear the floors and tie
the scarves around each other's waists
and hold each other, palm to palm
and cheek to cheek like lovers grown old
and slow in their love. They dance and the scarves
follow them through the night, beyond
the glass doors, beneath the stars,
amidst the houses full of flowers, flowers
smoother than the wind
that wraps itself around the turning world.

Think of the Blackouts

Think of the blackouts during the War.
Whole cities
Disappearing like flowers folding their petals at dusk
As if each town
Were lying down to sleep
In the arms of lost and hidden cities;
Sprawled beside Troy, nestled next to Pompeii,
Fallen across the arm of Atlantis breathing like a current.
And what is the pilot on his mission to think?
If only he can find his missing city
Twinkling below like an unspoken wish,
He and his crew will be whole again—
The pain in their backs disappear
Or their mothers be alive once more
Calling them in
From the gnat-thick evening . . .
Below, a river twists through the countryside
Where an occasional barge glitters like a firefly,
Meanders on the meandering river.
The pilot wonders if an error's been made.
Perhaps he's lost all orientation like a diver
And the stars above are the cities below
And he is sailing
Farther and farther from home,
Into the black night
Like a coin falling into a well,
Realizing that all he ever hoped for
Was a mistake, a miscalculation
On a map, the drone of the propellers

The failed prayer
Of a monk who sins, knows he sins,
And no longer cares.

Married Woman

Remember in "The Open Boat," the poor
bastards, so close, waving, screaming!
and the swimmers on the shore,
smiling and smiling, beaming
pink tourists along that stretch
of white sand waving back with all the good will
Christ meant them to have, the beach
and sky as vivid as a Homer painting? El,
I only read that story once but I still feel its horror.
And when I close my eyes I can still see your eyes
looking up into mine as clearly as I see that shore.
There is sorrow in shores, in boats, in swimming,
but especially in the love for a married woman.
They must have sickened at each pitch and rise.

Lot's Wife

Where will we be when something goes wrong?

When those men came to our house
I felt certain
their presence was a blessing—
the cattle would thicken
or the grass
return to the yard. Their skin
was so pretty and their teeth
good. When passing the bread
I touched one of their hands
and my body flushed as if a fire had spread
across my face, across the land.

I have heard the rabbis speak of angels.
On hot nights when we slept on the roof
I could almost see them,
connecting the stars
until faces and wings
spread before me in every direction.

What type of fire is it that rages so far away
that we might see it here? That that fire would touch our lives
as I touched his hand, like angels,
descending and descending
from every direction.

For L, Born August 6, 1945

A ring floats about your ankles
where the dew has soaked the circle

of your dress: a gray halo that sways
forward with the body displacing

the grass before it. When Newton
considered this world, the atom's

capacity to harbor light
was undreamed of; only its weight

and how it drew one body
to another the way God

would one day draw to his bosom
the scattered flock of his Chosen

as he descended to this planet,
terrible and effulgent.

Since then, science has
perfected its appliances

making the body-electric
almost palpable; atomic

and subatomic, so by 'forty-
five we could prepare a sortie

*

to glide slowly over Hiro-
shima and above ground-zero

release its burden.
                         On the wall
above our bed you've tacked a small

picture from that day. The photo
of a man, rather the shadow

of a man, who, when caught mid-stride
had his image thrown on the side-

walk before him as on a frame
of unexposed film.

Nothing remains of that man; not flesh
or muscle or bone or ash,

only that blackened silhouette
spread on the walk by the sudden white

flash that made his skeleton
shine for a moment through his skin

before he utterly disappeared.
It has now been forty-four years

since that day and we go on
with our lives as if nothing's wrong.

Tonight that photograph will shine
down on your empty dress like the moon
                    *

across a summer lake.
And again that picture will wake

you from your sleep and you'll press
yourself against me as if our flesh

were two halves of a greater whole,
the common vessel for each soul,

as if matter, divided, could bond
itself and heal forever the wound

that separates it.

II

Tolstoy on the Train to Astapovo

All night I watched myself watch myself in the window.
Stars and mountains and lights from a distant village rushed
through me, as I through them. Tired, I pushed
my face closer—half human, half shadow—
until my image disappeared from the glass
and only towns and mountains and the stars went past.

When I was young everything was sex,
and the pursuit of sex; the sleepy eyes
of peasant girls, daughters of Cossacks
and serfs, their mouths half-opened as if in praise

or to sing a love song in a foreign language.
Think of me as I'd like to; waking in an orchard
close to the ocean, the air full of apples and salt
and the sound of water.

When I wake now I'm exhausted with the knowledge
of my life and lie inside the tortured
bedding until morning counting faults
as if they were animals whose slaughter

could assuage the God I talk to and about.
But consider this: how even I who placed
that poor woman's head face-
down upon the tracks, wanted to shout
Stop, dear God, don't do it! refrained
and watched instead the inevitable train.

The Day Edward Hopper Left Home

Evening comes swift and hard, like an army,
and nowhere to hide. Inside
their houses children whisper prayers
and climbing in, cover themselves

to their necks. How long this wind
beneath the window? its shrill
incessant whistle . . . and this wound;
a father unshaven for three days,

still in his slippers, reading the same newspaper again
and again, and a mother who
does what he says. On the telephone lines
a little trembling seeps into the claws

of the birds returning to Canada,
a small pleasant tickle held deep inside,
like a secret that would send a man to jail
for many years.

The Reverend Falwell Describes
the Bakkers' Swimming Pool

It's been empty for a number of years,
   cracked in a hundred places by the chill
and thaw of the seasons. Now a smelly,
   thick, green water fills its deeper end
where large, mottled frogs, before they ascend
   from their mire, lay their eggs—a jelly
that hovers like the dark dream of a will-
   ful child, and would, if you let yourself near
enough, cling to every horrified inch
   of your skin reeking its sulphury stench.

I recall when its waters were as clear
   as the Jordan, sun-luminous and filled
nearly to overflow, casting fili-
   grees of light across the bottom and bend-
ing up along each wall. One could suspend
   both time and body here, immersed fully
in a world that defies the temporal
   and gravity's relentless pull. O fierce
the faith that keeps the soul and body drenched,
   and the apple still clinging to its branch.

Aleister Crowley Meets with the American Theosophists, Philadelphia, 1908

Dogs do not like him.
The room chills upon his entrance
And water evaporates
If he stays long enough.

It is not for love
(Nor is it hate
For that matter) that these trances
Possess him. His skin

Only serves to contain the din
His nerves make; snapping, trans-
ferring urgent but contained
Currents from one end of

His body to the other. If a cat were to rub
Against his leg, it would create,
Unknowingly, so enchanted,
A spark, so volatile and sudden

Its heart would stop and a hum
Like receding trains
Would pulse and vibrate
Where there had been organs and fluff.

*

Outside, thunder gathers above
Like angels grating
Their eyes in their sockets. A trace
Of ammonia fills the room. Something surely will happen.

Passenger Pigeons

All the passenger pigeons, dead.
Once so numerous, the sky
Darkened for hours as they plied
Their way across their American heaven. Audubon said

That when they roosted, the limbs
Cracked beneath, that it was impossible
To miss them with a gun. To cripple
Their mass or in the smallest way trim

Their number would have been like draining the ocean
Its water, though sometimes they could be knocked
From the sky merely by heaving a rock
Into their great vibrating motion.

Their dung fell like snow, covering the hills,
But lacking the romance of real snow,
Though it helped the crops grow
In the fall. But it ruined most of the wells

Which brought forth the sincerest oaths
But also an awe for all their mundane grandeur
From the farmers forced to endure
Their passing, which came to resemble only the gray blur of
    ghosts.

The Road-Gang Is Served Supper
at a Country Inn

In the kitchen mutton churns in the stew.
Basil dries from a string in the corner.
The convicts place their chins upon their blue
Shirts and mutter thanks. And now Molly has torn her
Skirt on a nail-head that juts out of
The cabinet, meant for the hanging of towels,
And so when she carries, balanced above
Each shoulder, the heaped and steaming bowls
Of food, her skirt flaps behind her like a flag
Above a beautiful and happy kingdom.
Outside, the world thickens in the slow drag
Of slanting light, while far away peals
The radiating bell of a church. Some
Men stare and listen. Others eat their meals.

An Incident at Andersonville
—from the Recollections
of Private Charles Hopkins

We formed the Regulators, a society
Of mutual protection, slept with an eye open
Or'd wake with our pockets gaping
Like a wound; the only propriety

Was staying alive day to day.
One morning their band of turncoats fell upon
A prisoner new to the camp, a Private Urban,
Whose mistake was to unwittingly display

A large roll of bills and a handsome watch.
Though beat half to death, he identified
One of his assailants who betrayed
Five of his cohorts. It took no time to catch

Them, whose only purpose in life,
It seemed, was to make ours more miserable.
But all were given a trial
(And an eloquent one, for lawyers were rife

Here, as was every profession and trade),
And eloquent or not, we found them guilty
And a gallows, six across and sturdy,
Was built right before their eyes, made

From a pine tree and six barrels—a throne
For each. And one by one, the barrels were kicked

Away and dropping fast, their necks cracked
Or they gasped for air as if choking on a bone.

And they hung there all day like sacrifices,
Like petitions to the Lord
That our lives be merely hard,
Or if he wouldn't help, leave us to our own devices.

Periodic

On *this* table how large
each symbol, and how seemingly stable—
Yet each element, like Mme DeFarge
ticking her needles, portends
a greater change. Jesus sups with friends,
by night they've cleared the table.

A Short History
of Christianity

Her water breaking any instant,
Nowhere to sleep, they found quasi-
Livable lodging in a town lousy
With travelers and gave birth to the infant

Between the cows and sheep. Gift-
Bearing kings arrived after-
ward burning incense to the rafters,
Bowing before the baby as they left

West atop their plodding camels.
Once when twelve, after a feast, he vanished
To his parents' dismay who managed
To retrace their steps back to the temple

To find him debating law with the rabbis. Later
He took up with publicans and sinners
Explaining Heaven, ate one last dinner
With his disciples (one was a traitor)

And was crucified and placed in a cave.   ·
In three days, rolling back the stone,
They claimed his body utterly gone,
Which the world does or doesn't believe.

A Scientist Aboard the Titanic
Says Good-Bye to His Wife
in His Head

Whatever goes up must come down; this is
a given. But what goes down does not nec-
essarily rise—never measure bles-
sings by expectation or aphorism.
A blessing much more resembles a gas,
is buoyant, is lighter than air, insists
on elevating both itself and its
subject past the common, much as a kiss
is able to do between wife and hus-
band or father and daughter. Osmosis,
however, is when a fluid—in this
case water—moves through a semiporous
membrane—such as the lungs—so that the pres-
sure is equalized. See how the ship lists
to one side like a man asleep in his
bed? All bodies seek a natural rest-
ing place; this is called homeostasis.
I had always thought mine land. I was mis-
taken.
          How strange this moon, white and quartered,
sets nothing on shore but light and water.

Weldon Kees
Drives to the Golden Gate

"The porchlight coming on again."
—W.K.

Stars stretched from here
to Baja and
my windshield suddenly appeared
radiant and vast,
while clouds as thin as a barely heard

conversation
lifted over
the bay where aluminum masts
rang like temple bells
against their halyards till the winds passed

and the boats bobbed
like kites above
their anchors. I drove past the well-
kept lawns and followed
the avenues leading through the hills

bayward in a
fog that blurred the
streetlamps, whose suspended dollops
of light, like flowers
reflected in a disturbed shallow,

shimmered before
each residence.

And in his house, late in these hours,
the insomniaced
husband tries to account for those powers

that shake his fridge
and rock his house
almost imperceptibly, back
all night long, and forth.
The night outside his window is black,

and if leaning
there, he can see
my lights approach and clear a path
dividing the world
in two: before and now, north and south,

those who sleep and
those who watch as
lights rise from the hill to herald
another false dawn,
crest the top and disappear like pearls

dropped back into
the sea. How strange
my lights must seem; up, down, then gone;
the light of the heart
on a cardiogram. Driving on

I watched his porch-
light sink and rise,
like a man drowning, then depart
upward from my mirror
once and for all.
However charted,

*

35

the world revolves
around our own
bright lights, so it was never clear
if he yawned then stepped
satisfied from bed to bed to hear

his kids breathing
and then retired
beside his generous wife to sleep
soundly until noon.
Nor could he know how my car had crept

quietly to
the shoulder, or
from his soft dreams would he presume
how my clock emptied
itself before me as the big moon

empties itself
of light, the sky
turning blue, as the stars, plenty
and luminous, stir
and pale, and dumbly disassemble.

The Awful Balance

When my grandfather was dying,
my mother would read to him his favorite passage:
Only this evening I saw again low in the sky
The evening star, at the beginning of winter, the star
That in spring will crown every western horizon,
Again . . .
And since his memory was like an empty shelf
she read the same piece each day
and he took delight in it over and over.
And just as a sailor turns a stone in his mouth
to slake his thirst,
my grandfather turned the words
until they slid from the morphined pillow of his brain.

Once the stars had risen
she'd place him by the bay windows
where his body filled with salt air.
And though too cold, it no longer mattered,
its comfort greater than its threat, the breeze
pressing itself upon him as easily as sleep a child,
and his eyes, refusing no world,
told us he was still half here
and so half elsewhere.

Vermeer also placed those he loved most
by open windows, allowing the light from without
to illuminate his subjects' faces
nearly as much as by their own quiet domesticity.
How many times did that woman read that letter
repeating those phrases that made her most happy

until remembering a meal needed preparing
or water fetching
she folded the letter and placed it in her blouse
thinking no further of it but allowing
its presence about her moving body
to make each chore simple and pleasurable?

The awful balance, Ellie, fearing
that which we love most will be taken from us
and never return. I imagine now that he has returned
growing large inside your belly. When I kiss your eyes
and you say my name over and over
we are on a raft,
the perfect shift of weight
keeping us afloat.
Your eyes the blue of her blouse, the color of the sailor's sky.

That Your Hands
Are Graceful and Kind

for Ellie

You left the overhead light on which burned
all night, till nearly morning, when Cedar
woke crying, perhaps hungry, and you turned
from your place next to me to feed her
if necessary, but mostly to let
her know that you were beside her and God
was in his heaven. Is it light that prods
us from our sleeping? Surely light begets
light and pulls us, as an infant is pulled
from the birth canal into waiting hands;
hands whose shapes are defined by that child's shape
and in turn, define for that child, the world.
There's little of this world I understand.
Only that your hands are graceful and kind
    and lie like light across my chest while I sleep.

Mayflies

"A given distance can be halved ad infinitum."
—Zeno's Dichotomy

They use assiduously their given time,
Some texts say twenty-four hours,
Others ten or twelve. In World War I
When flying was novel enough
That bombs were dropped by the pilot's own hand,
My grandfather, watching from above,
Tried to follow their graceless descent
Tracing the long golden section described
Till they flashed, white and silent,
The way serotonin does
On some hillside of the brain.
Later at the university, when he taught
How the wide array of the animal kingdom
Flew, crawled, or swam themselves
Toward the unseen glory
That willed their locomotion,
He spoke of the mayfly, how its heart
Was proportionately the same size
As the human's and beat
In such furious synch with the blurred wings
It could, were it large enough, induce seizure
In an epileptic. Such timing, he explained,
Allowed a machine gun to be mounted
On the nose of a biplane
And never shoot its own propellers.

The mayfly, if extrapolated to human terms,
Would live to be eighty.

It is the first cool night of autumn, 1964.
My grandfather tells me
There is less space between the two stars
That float above us like shy teenagers
Than between any two electrons
Whirling within the heart.
This, I think, is how love works—
Were I to ride light, like some angelic
And fevered horse, the great arc of space
Like the shell of the tortoise that holds the world,
Would forever bring me back here to myself.
And I think I understand—how a circuit once completed
Has no beginning nor end and we, like Zeno's runner,
Live forever between here and there, between the lubb and
    dubb
Of the beating heart, arising once and always,
Like Jesus, incorruptible, from the cave. And all around us
The air is hushed but for two crickets
Calling back and forth, tiny and splendid,
Across the chilling night.

IV

The Fishermen
Pull Their Boats In

The green hills spill to the beach
and the fishermen pull their boats in,
light as souls while on the water,
a burden on land where the prows
furrow the sand, and like spent animals,
rest all night on their sides.
Sometimes teenagers lie between the hulls,
whispering and drunk, the big-handed boys
astonished by their good fortune, the fine hair
on her leg rising again after his hand,
five fingers happy as a choir. Some mornings

the fishermen find cast-off rubbers,
small exhausted fish, their ridiculous wrinkled bodies
pointing back to the water into which the boats
heave themselves each August
full of light and coffee and sandwiches,
and don't return for days. No trace of them,
freshly painted white and trimmed with red. And no trace
of their wives' footprints,
or of the sand-angels the teenagers made,
their delicate ribs and scapulas
swimming, a fine salt gown
on their skin where the sweat
evaporated as it rose to the clouds
before falling again to the sea.

The Grown Children
of Dead Parents

Their white markers
rise like loaves
each evening,
cooling in the dark,

and their well-dressed
children listen there for a reminder
or a recipe lost in the wind,
so that they must press

their hands behind their ears,
tilting and squinting.
The moon rises, tinting
the clouds like a bruise,

and the children button
a top button against the weather—
"... *you will never* ...
something" and then "*something* ..."

Snow in Miami, 1977

Those clouds
were an unknown dark, not the purple

of our summer downpours
but an uncatalogable gray like the color

of a half-recalled dream in which something
is explained and satisfies the sleeper

who cannot carry it back
to wakefulness. The moon

swathed the pale buildings in a white so quiet
you'd have swaddled a baby in it while the stars

turned and turned above the house. It was beautiful
and stretched forever, the air so clear

that each lit window across the field
was a sail full of wind, a polar wind.

And half-asleep you could hear the voice
of one who loved you years ago, who loved you

no matter what. *Darling,* it said,
Please close the door, it's cold, it's so cold.

Childhood Bathtub

Whiter than ivory,
Wider than a smile,
The waves lap the miles
And I let every
One of them carry
Me to a farther
Island till Father
Calls in to bear me
Back to this one, this
Shore and the drain's whorl.
Outside, the darkness
Fills the empty world.

Owl and Mouse in a Cage

Hand-fed milk from a dropper, then worm-meal
from the tip of a spoon, they've been companions
since birth, as if nature had crossed wires
as it does occasionally in serial killers
or presidents who spent too much
of their youth in the sun. They take their turns
at the small upturned water bottle, like Oliver Hardy
moving a piano with Mme Defarge
or Romulus looking to find Uncle Remus beside him
at the foot of Rome's third eternal hill.
The literature attests to a long history
of such anomalous couplings. Think of Miss Hershmeyer
who paired us, boy girl boy girl: a dozen
young men with small erections
pummeling Johann Strauss into submission, a row
of burred heads nestled as closely as possible between
the dozen small valleys of upturned breasts,
listening for a deeper relay of jungle drums, for
some clue, as if our individual genetic codes
would be broken down and set to music right there
in those outstretched arms. No clue.
Only the thinning sunlight of the doors swung wide
onto Le Jeune and the day too far gone
except to go home, change clothes, and play tag
with the dog until the heat quivered upward
out of the asphalt and a siren
rose above the antennaed roofs, held for a second
like Caruso on the scratched seventy-eight,
and then was gone and I came in for dinner
with parents who didn't know better,

who were young even then,
who loved each other but didn't know better
and who would come apart like a china plate
painted with wild roses, sliding
from the grip of someone's soapy hands.

Lament

When a woman unfastens her skirt for a man
And lifts above her head her shirt
So he can smooth the triangle of hair
That is a harbor below the belly
And place his tongue against
The nipples firm with blood,
She moans and without knowing it
Makes him believe that age will never dry
His already half-dry bones
Or the rain overwhelm in flood.
If you were here
I would forgive myself and change.

I could taste the butter dried
In the corners of your mouth.
Behind each ear my fingers
Listened to your pulse, and your cunt
Swelled gathering glory to itself, a basket of flowers
In disarray. But do not mistake love
For the reasons of love.
Listen to my heart, like a man with one crutch,
Crying Help me Help me.
Outside, the wind turns fierce and strange.
If you were here I would forgive myself,
I would forgive myself and change.

Near and Far

—St. Agnes's Eve; Loxahatchee Orange Groves

Nights turn clear when the mercury
drops suddenly this way, or until the smudge-
pots are lit, and then the sky's a circle
out of Dante, an oily smoke surging

from a fire that bobs across my face
and throws my shadow in the thorny branches.
It's Sunday once more and you're in your place
and I'm here, miles away. On a map it's inches.

But peeling this orange, as Mercator
once did to represent the world,
the poles splay and only the equator
remains intact. How, from a fruit uncurled

with a knife, do we calculate the distance?
Later this morning you'll rise and plunge
into the tub, then turn on the kitchen's
tabletop radio and peel an orange

yourself, bringing sections one by one to your mouth
so that Zeno's proven wrong by your sure hand
and simple will. Yet I'm still south
and you north and the distance is spanned

only by our good wishes. Near and far
are undone only here, in the dark, where my torch

seems brighter than any of the stars
I search the sky for and makes the leaves, arched

above my head, glow like a wide
passage. And for a moment I am Porphyro
making my way back to Madeline's side,
to you, and I almost hear the radio

you turn from station to station
searching the dial for a favorite song
as a man scans the sky for a constellation
before it wheels from the trees and is gone.

Your Voice

Whatever they were saying through the walls
neither of us could hear, only the hum and pitch
their talking took, like the rumbling a car makes
shifting gears before it negotiates
a hill. We knew their marriage was bad and listened
to each plaintive lilt twist in the air
beyond the counterpoint of their radio until
only her crying was left. One summer,

after our last fight, we lost our dog
and combed the streets for hours calling his name.
Your voice, even then, full of fear,
was lovely. And at a distance, the name obscured,
I could hear your one note carry across
the neighborhoods filling with dark,
like the whistle that allowed my father
to come home each day where he closed his eyes
before dinner, and unable to sleep or not sleep,
rehearsed again what he planned to say
and again would not.

What could I have said that you'd have understood,
that wasn't foolish, or disgraced
with the obvious? That my name
on those nights you tried to ease me into sleep
would not have bent a flame? That I fought sleep,
as Jacob did the angel, so I could listen
again and again.

V

The Idiot Savants

They remind us
that civilizations
perished
before recorded history,
that the moon
is so slow across the pampas
we mark its
passage
only by where it is
no longer.
The blind boy
with the lumbering gait
who turns his face
to the starry night
and rolls
his head from side
to side limning
the infinite
spaces he sees within,
plays
the piano
as if an angel had
kissed each palm before
singing in his ear.
Darwin said
each incremental
generation
of change
begets the next,
adapting to the

peculiar circumstances
that dictate
its existence.
Gould maintains
that evolution
is random aberration,
a cluster of cells
whose nuclei
burst like a bunch of roses
turning toward
an unseen
sun.

In the morning,
light filters
through your hair
and falls along
your sleeping face.
The signals in the brain
slow from beta
to delta and the brain
relaxes its hold, curls
about itself like a cat
on the windowsill
the first warm day
after a hard winter.
How and *Why*
melt like snow
and can't be applied

to the dark-skinned boy
forming
a water buffalo
from a handful of clay,

his only model a photograph
in *National Geographic*
shiny and two-
dimensional. The animal
pulls an empty cart
down a dusty road,
two children
walk behind. The detail
is exquisite
in his small hands.
I don't know

how this is possible
how grace's
stubborn osmosis
permeates each cell,
covers the brain
like a diadem
of clouds
above the fields
and rutted lanes
where the two children
walk home, the rain
that breaches the soil
penetrating
each stem.

Chemistry

Whatever synapse-leaping chemical
triggers response—finger from the hot stove
or the memory of a friend twenty years
dead—would, if poured from a beaker,
eat a hole through pig-iron. Quicker
than rust but slower than the sheer
beam of laser, it's searing, chimerical,
thorough; in many ways resembles love.

Asleep Together

Last night before the night-sounds
had risen from the lawn, and silence
lay across the lake like fog,

we watched a gray gull coast
through the gray light until it was gone,
and lay down to sleep naked

beneath the brown blankets, coasting
on our own exhaustion away from the ballast
of the body. Outside, a vagrant cat

got locked in the shed behind
the azalea row and we dreamed of a baby
crying off and on until morning.

In winter when the water has frozen,
no longer a window or mirror, I've watched
a dozen cats chase the vague

silhouettes the fish make
below. Bewildered, they slide beyond
their destinations, their imperfect gyres

like strange maverick stars
forming new constellations
in the black and endless heaven.

Tonight the tethered moon rolls
above us in its place. Gravity
soaks our sleeping limbs. We turn

*

to one another, the delicate orbit
that holds us face to face, and swim
concentric paths. The air is quiet

and full of warmth. It must appear
that we listen to the planet turn,
eyes lowered, ears toward the earth.

In the Kitchen

The windows grow small with frost and the moon
Is large above the house. On the baby's hands
Are red socks, curled above his face.
Far away, a siren or a dog.
In your long hair is a trellis of flowers
Which makes everything in the kitchen brighter.
It defies all sensemaking, the weather so cold
And the south so far away. You try not to draw
Attention to yourself, but how can you help it?
Here, drink some more wine. We have warmed some wine
And though it's good wine, we put an apple in it.
Here, setting the wine before me. But I don't want more wine.
I want to ask about the flowers. He wakes up
And his red hands sink deep into your yellow hair.

The Island of Glassblowers

There are seventeen words for sand here.
Every schoolchild
Knows the increments in the arc of a sparrow's flight,
Such figures determining the thickness of glass.

Along the western walls of these white houses
Cheese is found in gauze
Suspended from a string running beneath the eaves.
Cats sleep, listening
For the drip of whey beside their heads.
This pose—a cat sleeping—
Adorns the mouth of the small harbor in glass
Which a play of light makes opaque by day
But shines at night outward to the sailors returning home
From seas which themselves
Are as smooth as glass.

By the time a boy is fourteen
He learns to work the furnaces.
His fingers
Become a shade darker than the rest of his hands
And are a source of pride called "abhroterra"—
"Stones from a field of glass" or "That which is valuable like a
    diamond."

A house of mirrors was established here in 1697
Where a master's mistakes could be displayed
And painted black on one side.
The short come here to become tall,
And the thin fat, and their good-hearted laughter

Is heard all over the grounds
Where families picnic on Sundays
And find sand in their salads,
Making parents smile at their children
For God's unknowable wisdom.

This Afternoon

This afternoon Mr. Bennington's horses
pushed through a break in the fence
and wandered to the harbor. Then,
too delighted to leave, exhilarated and pacified
by the sun over the bay and the breeze,
they waited for Mr. Bennington
to come and retrieve them, scolding them,
shaking his head. Small clods of earth
marked where they had run.

Down by the docks the pale flowers
float toward the sawmill.
It appears in this moonlight as if the girls
of Mrs. Yakamoto's Sunday school class
had taken off their hats
and cast them on the river,
watching them drift into the almost black night.
The girls say nothing. You say nothing.

From here you can see the bed sheets of the Wyndmere Hotel
hung out to dry, flapping.
It's as if an orchestra of blind men
were setting up to play, just beyond the hill.
No need for them to turn pages,
you falling asleep beside me.

My Grandfather
Recalls His Wrong Answer

The night in that planetarium
twenty-four years ago shivered
and flashed, the heavens a delirium
of lights spiraling above

as the rotating projector rained
sparks across the curved ceiling
like neurons firing along the brain
of a suddenly happy man, until reeling

about us, a whole year pivoted
before our eyes in less than an hour.
And as each star unriveted
itself from the walls ending our tour

of the skies, her face masked
in the half-dispersed
dark, she turned to me and asked,
which of us, years from now, would be first.

Moving Away

Socrates chose death to exile,
Too tired to pull the long and tethered chain of the familiar
Through the landscape of the unfamiliar.
Or consider the way a man can hold to his chest
A woman who is not the woman he loves.
Or live with the fear of waking
Day after day in some strange field
Counting the rows as if they were years,
Breath as tattered as cornstalk.

I drove to the house yesterday
Forgetting I'd moved.
No one there to stumble out
Squinting and dumbfounded
Smiling into the white afternoon.
Sometimes late at night your absence
Fills the terrible question mark
Of the body and I think how human it is
That we can sweep a hand before our eyes
And change the color of the day
Or the meaning of a conversation within our heads
But how the heart
Continues to repeat itself.

For what we call home is not home.
The crowds, shopping,
Eating at the drugstore, watching themselves
Like ghosts in the store windows,
At night their feet propped upon chairs

Ready for bed,
Mistaken.

But that body which presupposes the body,
Tethered to the sleeping body
Only by a cord of breath and light,
Travels where it may
Through the sticky air in this city of fronds.
That same breath which travels between us,
That unreels so magnificently
That transparent kite of light,
Animates these bodies
Which so easily found home in one another.
For what we call home is not home,
It is our breath I remember
Creating a home around us,
A bed before us,
Washing each other's faces
Like an otherworldly light,
Your eyes full of disbelief and grateful,
The empty cups of the lungs
Filling themselves again and again
Illuminating our tired hearts
More brightly
Than the cities of our birth.

"Passenger Pigeons" is after William Heyen's poem "Pigeons."

A fuller account of the story told in "An Incident at Andersonville—from the Recollections of Private Charles Hopkins," as related by Private Hopkins, is in *American Heritage,* October/November 1982.

The passage quoted in "The Awful Balance" is from Wallace Stevens's "Martial Cadenza."

"Near and Far," "Your Voice," "The Idiot Savants," and "Asleep Together" were written for L. R.

Steve Kronen is a licensed massage therapist
and teaches English part-time at
Miami Dade Community College.

The Contemporary Poetry Series
Edited by Paul Zimmer

The Contemporary Poetry Series
Edited by Bin Ramke